A VOICE Crying In The Wilderness

OWN YOUR MESSAGE AND STAND IN YOUR TRUTH

Pauline-Elizabeth Grant

Published By

P E A C H E S

P U B L I C A T I O N S

Published by Peaches Publications, 2022.
www.peachespublications.co.uk
The moral right of the author has been asserted.

Unless otherwise noted, Scripture quotations are taken from the King James
Version (KJV). Public Domain.

British Library Cataloguing in Publication Data: A catalogue record for this
book is available from the British Library.

ISBN: 9798463089342.

Book cover design: Johnathan Butler/Peaches Publications.
Front cover photography: Tasha Peeters.
Back cover photography: Ryan Haven from rockandstone4tography.
Editor and Proofreader: Linda Green.
Typesetter: Winsome Duncan.

Reflections on Becoming Me

HOW HAVE I CHANGED

My confidence has grown
More patient and calm
I`ve stepped out of my comfort zone
To share my life experience

I can feel my growth
I can hear my growth
I can see my growth

I know I belong
I am not waiting to become
I am enjoying being me
I feel free

I can feel my growth
I can hear my growth
I can see my growth

I don`t feel condemned because of my decisions

I have arrived
I am sensitive to God`s voice
I am a lifelong learner

I can feel my growth
I can hear my growth
I can see my growth

No Other Me

There will never be another me
No one can ever do
what God has graced me to do
It`s time for me to walk into
My God-given destiny
The time is now
All wrapped up in my confidence
With Gods love, I can keep going
There will never be another me

Belong

Knowing that I belong
Knowing that I am no longer out of place
Knowing I don`t need to fit in, I was born to stand out

Knowing that it`s my time to arise and shine
Knowing that I am beautiful
Knowing that I am fearfully and wonderfully made

Knowing that I have arrived
Knowing that I have stepped in
Knowing that I have the right to press the pause button

Knowing that I can`t turn back
Knowing that people are waiting for me
Knowing that it`s okay if I don`t get it all right

Knowing that it`s okay not to be ok
Knowing that it`s okay to say no
Knowing that it`s okay to ask for help and to be me

I Will

Whatever is in my heart
I will feel it
Whatever is in my life
I will live it
Whatever has come my way
I'll deal with it
What God destines me to be,
I will be it

Contents

Contents

Dedication

I dedicate this book to my daughter Tasha and son Selvin
who patiently journeyed with me and allowed me to find
myself as I transitioned through my pain.

May this book empower you to own your voice,
as you grow towards becoming the best version
of yourselves.

Acknowledgements

I thank my daughter-in-law Remiee for the consistency of love she showed me. Thanks to my five grandchildren: Raya, Layth, Mya-Bella, Dieudonne and Aaleyah, who allowed me to be a glamour mama who is always studying. I thank my mum who was patient and tolerated me when I was in my angry withdrawal season. Family, you allowed me to work on myself and overcome the hurdle that had me stuck in silence and fear. I now live my truth, which enables me to be happy and free with who I have become.

I acknowledge my six church Spiritual Mothers who have journeyed with me these past twenty-nine years. Mum Esther, Mum Edith, and Anne R.I.P, Mum Beckles, Mum Mathews and Mum Rose continue to journey with me. These six mothers have held my hand, prayed for and with me, laughed and cried with me during my good and bad days. Supported me with my children and taught me how to be a mother and a wife even when I didn`t want to listen because of my pain.

I am grateful for the leadership of:

CLC church with Bishop Wayne Malcolm, for the foundation of my Christian journey, where I was able to launch R.O.O.T.S Prayer Ministry;

Arc Church Pastor Peter Nembhard at the middle of my Christian journey, I was able to hide and grow in R.O.O.T.S;

New Jerusalem Church Pastor Yvonne Brookes where I worship now, as I can explore being a woman positioned in the Kingdom for a time such as this.

These churches have enhanced my spiritual growth as I was able to grow through my pain on my Christian journey over these twenty-nine years. I now see the pleasure in my journey and have nothing but gratitude for my yesterday.

I acknowledge motivational speakers and transformational coaches such as: Maya Angelou, Madam C J Walker R.I.P, Les Brown, Lisa Nichols, Mel Robbins, Andy Harrington and Iyanla Vanzant, as I celebrate their authenticity and how they show the pain in their stories which is very empowering and impactful. They have enabled me to own my life experience and see them all as gifts that I needed.

I celebrate my spiritual support team: my spiritual mother Vivienne Downes; my spiritual father and overseer Steven Samuels; and, my spiritual daughter Emelia Aimey. They work alongside me, allowing that which is on the inside to ooze out. They have corrected and nurtured me in love. I constantly felt built up and not torn down. They allowed me to catch my breath when at times I was drowning in my pain. They constantly held out a lifeline, telling me: 'to keep going', 'don`t stop', 'I had their blessing', 'that it was ok to be me', and 'to follow my instinct/ my dream/vision'. Even though at times I didn`t know what I was doing, I trusted God's leading and He always came through for me.

I celebrate Lady Karen Allen for being a role model, as a female teacher/ Preacher of the gospel your authentic and transparent style of delivering Gods word from your heart and personal experience always leaves me captivated and encouraged to be the best version of myself in and out of the church. Thank you, Karen, for paving the way for me to own my voice, you have taught me to step out of the box.

I give acknowledgement to Pastor Yvonne Brookes for the 10 weeks of Project Be women empowerment sessions, which inspired me to write my reflection poem.

I also acknowledge the late Maya Angelou for her autobiography *And Still I Rise*, from the Author of *I Know Why The Caged Bird Sings*, printed and bound in Great Britain in 1984 by Virago Press, London. Your words and your story inspired me.

All Biblical quotes are from on less otherwise stated.

I would like to acknowledge and thank my daughter Tasha who took photos of my granddaughters to reflect and illustrate 'see no evil, speak no evil, hear no evil', of the days when I felt voiceless.

Finally, I acknowledge you, my reader friend, for receiving this book and I trust you will use it as a sign post, to enable the transitioning from pain to pleasure, whilst you Own Your Voice.

Only those who really care about you can hear you when you are silent.

By Eagle[1]

---

[1] The Meaning of Life, Eagle (15 April 2020) "Only those who care about you, can hear you when you're quiet.", Internet cited on 13.12.2021 at: https://timelesslife.info/only-those-who-care-about-you-can-hear-you-when-youre-quiet

Foreword

Preacher, Minister, author, Book Angel for WOW book club

I have had the privilege to journey with Pauline - Elizabeth Grant as her book angel as she was putting her book together. And I have had the opportunity to see first-hand what an amazing author she is. Her life story put within each line of her book will not only encourage you, but will awaken the giant that's sleeping within you; you will slowly begin to realize that there is more to you than the limitations that the world's system, the strong holds in your mind, and your surrounding circumstances have imposed on you, therefore shutting the voice of your identity. Pauline – Elizabeth is a gifted storyteller who, at this point in her life, is driven by the deep desire to see a generation empowered and encouraged to live in their truth, stepping into their God-designed identity and purpose. I am fully convinced that by the time you finish reading this book, something would have shifted inside you, and you will be equipped to live in your truth and be the best version of yourself.

Samuel DvinKitenge

Introduction

This book is a reflection of my life from childhood into my adult life. It shows how I listened to my negative chatter and the lies I told myself about myself. Self-care has enabled me to appreciate self-love. Not owning my voice and speaking my truth, was an unconscious decision that I made. Now I know, I am using my voice to empower myself and hopefully you will have your own personal experience, as you journey with me through the pages of this book.

I grew up in the late 1950s in the UK and did not enjoy the winters. I can see myself as a little girl sitting behind the front room door leaning against the wall near the radiator to keep myself warm. I remember I refused to wear a slip, (Jamaicans call it a petticoat) under my dress or skirt as I saw it as another skirt, yet I was always cold. My mum didn`t know, as when I was a teenager she often left for work or came in from work when I had already left for school. I am of Jamaican parents that arrived in the UK in the late 1950s, who came for 5 years intending to return to Jamaica. But once married and children arrived, the goal post changed. Working hard and buying a house in the UK became the goal.

I was that quiet, yet happy go lucky little girl who was the sandwich between two brothers. Tony was two years older, R.I.P, and

Christopher two years younger who lives in the UK. My parents, especially my mother, worked hard, and I thought that was the way of life. Jamaican proverb "If you want good, your noise have to run". I grew up hearing a lot of proverbs, "money don't grow on trees", was one of them. My brothers and I learnt to earn money quite early. We sang in Holy Trinity Anglican Church Choir in Mile End and got paid; we got paid more when we sang at a wedding. We loved doing carol singing, we mastered it, and went on our own and kept the money. We didn't tell mummy and daddy; that was our extra pocket money. In fact, my parent's didn't need to give us pocket money. Doing part-time jobs on the stall in Roman Road market was a big thing in those days, or sewing buttons on clothes in the factory at Whitechapel are what I remember doing with my friends Elizabeth Simons and Pauline Roach. My parent's also had their way of hustling, by keeping parties in the basement. A party was called "a blues". Oh, how I loved the reggae music, especially the pirate ones that came straight from Jamaica! I can smell and taste the curry goat and patties now; can you? Looking back on my childhood my parents knew how to socialise. Food and music was an essential part of their lifestyle.

Looking back, and I want you to look back with me, I wasn't protected. In their busyness to earn money and provide for the family in UK and Jamaica they were not watching me. It is the grace of God that I wasn't sexually abused, raped by several men, abducted or killed. For a little girl, I had too much liberty, too much freedom. Too much time on my hands to think, and tell myself lies about what I thought people were saying.

At 13 I became a handful; I became promiscuous I met a boy at the Anglican church he was 17 years old. I don't recall hearing my parents say they loved me. I believe they thought by providing food, clothes, a roof over our heads, that said it all. Well, it didn't.

I don't blame them, well not now. I don't believe they heard it from their parents.

I admire my granddaughter's Raya and Mya-Bella, as they can plait and twist their hair. My daughter Tasha learnt to plait her hair at an early age. I can't plait or twist my hair and always wondered why, yet never even made the effort. Yet I like my hair styled nicely especially when I go to the hairdressers. Saturday 3rd July 2021, yes! this year. I was on a long-distance video WhatsApp call with my mum and I showed her Mya–Bella combing her hair. I asked why as a little girl I didn't learn to plait my hair. My mum said as a little girl she was not allowed to comb her hair. Her cousin my aunty Norma could do it or her grandmother Ma. It is strange, mummy did say this before, but the "penny has just dropped". Do you remember that proverb? I told you I was a proverbs girl.

I feel somewhat robbed and left out, because I believe, every little girl should be able to plait her hair. I did learn to plait my dolls hair but that wasn't the same. I recall wearing little wigs and afro puffs, do you remember the afro puffs? My mum did hair dressing as a side hustle, and I was her model, then they called it "genuine pig". Anyway, I felt like a little woman when I was a little girl. I was in primary school, getting on the train all on my own at the age of 11. Scary! I wouldn't even let my daughter or grandchildren go up the road on their own. I hear you saying "we are in different times".

The difference is if anyone attempted to touch my daughter or granddaughters inappropriately, they would speak up. My generation and especially my mum's generation would not say anything. For starters no one would believe, it was normal to "sweep things under the carpet" Couples didn't get divorced they tolerated things for the sake of keeping the family together. I know many of you can relate to what I am saying.

I choose not to call any names, but on reflection, there were two males who I have always questioned myself about. I keep saying, "Did they touch me when I was a little girl?" The thought has never left me. I have always wanted to know the truth, but would never do hypnosis. I am now ready to do psychotherapy because I believe it is my right to know the truth. I am no longer that little girl who is scared to ask questions; scared of opening the can of worms. I am A Voice Crying in the Wilderness who has come to set myself free, and as many families that are ready to Own their Voice and Speak their truth while setting generations free.

It is good to look back. I always liked clothes and as a little girl at early secondary school age around age 11, I did a modelling course. For the photo shoot, I had to apply my make-up. At that age, I knew nothing about make-up, in fact, I still don't. There was I at the photo shoot applying my make-up. Some girls had their mothers, others knew how to apply makeup. When I saw the developed photos I was so embarrassed, I looked like a clown, and my brother Christopher made me feel worse. He laughed at me. I decided I wasn't going to bother with modelling, the agency only wanted my mum's money, I lost my passion. For years every time I looked at the photos in my mind I could see and hear my brother Christopher laughing at me. He used to tell family and friends how horrible the photos were. When living in Jamaica I did a Fashion Design course, at Duffs Business college, I also had to model the garments I designed and made. I was grateful they helped me with the makeup. I did a Nancy Tailor finishing course.

While writing this book, I was reminded that as an author it is required to put a photo on the cover. I must admit I was reluctant, as I had the flash back from my childhood. How many of you understand the importance of building rapport and trusting people? Well,

I trusted Nadine Haven the makeup artist and her husband Ryan Haven the photographer who I know from the Arc church in London. They came to Birmingham and I was like "putty in their hands". I felt so comfortable, "the proof is in the pudding". As I look at my photo. I could see how confident I had become. I was shocked! I didn't even recognise myself. WOW! WOW! WOW! I felt like an over-50 model. What do you think, I look good for a 63-year-old author, don't I?

My reader, what dream can you resurrect? What lies have you been telling yourself? Who needs to hear your voice, your story? Please let your story be your legacy, the book the world can have the opportunity to read?

... If God is for us, who can be against us?

Romans 8:31 (NIV)

CHAPTER 1

I Was Lost

I was lost. When I was a little girl my mum said *"Children should be seen and not heard"*. So, here am pouring my heart out as a little girl at the age of 11, to you.

I believe some of you may understand what it feels like to be in a crowd and it feels like no one can see or hear you. Yet you are wearing bright colours so that you can be seen. I went to secondary school wearing a stripped top expecting my teacher to say something, but she didn`t. I wanted her to telephone my mum. But she didn`t. I felt lost in school and at home. I believe some of you can relate to what it`s like to be in a crowd and still feel lost. I thought I was meant to fit in with the crowd, now I understand God meant for me to stand out. The word of God states "I am fearfully and wonderfully made" (Psalm 139:14 NIV) I didn`t know this then. I understand now that I am unique. I felt like a child in an adult's body, it felt like I was meant to cope with life and whatever came being born in the 1950s. It felt like nobody understood, they didn`t ask me how I felt, what I thought, I was just expected to be seen and not heard, but I felt lost. I was lost in a family that was dealing with the mental wellbeing of my brother Tony. The only thing is we never spoke as a family about his health.

Looking back now there was a denial. But what was I to say, who was I to speak?

I would like you to come on a journey with me, while I speak through my colours, I didn't know I had the right to ask my family any questions, about the family.

I loved my family but they didn't know I was shy and had low self-esteem. I didn't know I was shy and had low self-esteem. I didn't even know what everyone called 'shyness' was low self-esteem. Journey with me back into my childhood. If you can relate, did you know about low self-esteem? So, I didn't get the attention I was seeking from my family, especially my mum, who was a hard-working wife and nurse. Question to you my reader, did you come from a family where your mum was busy trying to help the immediate and extended family? My mum worked a second job.

I admired my mum, but my admiration turned to hate because I wanted her company. I wanted her to spend more time with me. So, what was I really craving? I was craving her love and attention.

So, what did I do? Guess? Let me tell you since you can't guess. I got myself a boyfriend. Yes, I got myself a boyfriend, you heard me right.

I went to my parents and said I had met a boy at church. Yes, I met a boy at church, and guess what my parents said. No, they didn't say "Paul you are too young, you are only 12 years old.".

They said, "Bring him home."

Oh yes, they did. So, I brought him home. He was 17 years old.

Then after a matter of days, my parents decided I was too young to have a boyfriend.

I thought, "What, too young! Why didn't you say that in the first place?

I didn't say this out loud, I was thinking it in my head. "The horse has bolted, and you want to pull it back."

My little heart was broken, because you know what, I thought by having a boyfriend, I had someone to love me and give me attention. I thought my world had fallen apart. Oh yes, that's how it felt.

I was so angry with my parents, especially my mum. She had a stronger voice than my dad. So, you know what, I took an overdose. I felt life was not worth living. This was far from the truth. Why was I feeling lost? Looking back I felt lost in my little make-believe world of what I believed a family should be like. Father goes to work and mother stays at home to look after the kids.

If my mum was at home more, maybe this would have blocked me from doing the mischievous things I did, like staying in bed and going to school late. Going to school signing my name and left, then spent the day on the train with my boyfriend, saying I was going to typing classes but went to the cinema instead.

I don't think my parents knew anything about me, I could show them typing work that I did months ago, which was undated. My parents were so tired, I showed it to them when they were in bed. They said "Well done". However, it was clear they hadn't checked my work.

This is why I am so glad my daughter and daughter-in-law have the time to check on my grandchildren.

... I have placed before you an open door that no one can shut. ...

Revelations 3:8 (NIV)

CHAPTER 2

Things or time

I am a pre-teenager, a very sad one. I love to dance, it makes me feel happy, I am 12, but nobody knows that my dancing was part of a quest to be seen by my family and their friends. If I told you, would you believe that I was trying to get your attention mummy?

Michael Jackson was born on the same birthday and same year as me, so I lived in a very colourful and lively era. I have always loved wearing bright colours, having my hair done, having my nail polished, and I loved bright coloured shoes, but it was also part of my struggle to be seen and heard.

My whole persona was tied up in a cry of "Can you see me? If you did, why didn`t you say hello? Why did you pass me by? Why didn`t you call me? If you had, my Mum and Dad or brothers would have told me you called to say hi."

It felt like you didn`t care about me. You were that adult who was too busy for a youngster. Or should I say you were too busy for me? Well, that`s how it felt. I loved going to the youth clubs and family parties. Even as I got older, I loved going to parties and clubs, but you know what, even though I was in a building full of people I still felt alone.

If my mum took me to family or friends parties she would always say, "Dance."

I didn't want to dance especially when I was in primary school. I remember that well. Mummy would say "Dance" but if I didn't she would say "Dance or I'll pinch you."

Today it would be classed as emotional abuse. I didn't want to be pinched so I danced.

I know now why mummy wanted me to dance, it allowed her to look good. I remember when I became a mum, and my daughter Tasha was little. I didn't have to say dance, and when she did dance it made me feel good. So, I know exactly how my mum felt when I danced. I was, and still am, a good dancer. Dancing raised my joy level, I go into my happy place. When dancing I see no one it's like I enter another realm and I am comfortable just being me.

I remember my mum would always buy new clothes and would send me to church. She didn't go because she was tired from the night shift as a nurse, and she had to prepare dinner. Mummy would always say "Did they like your clothes, Paul?" It was your way to show me off, your way to show yourself as a good provider and a good mother, but you were not there for me, mum.

I did feel good in my nice new clothes, they made me feel special, as I always looked the best. So, I blame my mummy for the clothes and daddy for the music and dancing.

I learnt to speak through my clothes and my dancing, they were the ways I expressed myself, but nobody realised my loneliness and feeling of being abandoned. Even when we arrived home from school you were not there. We fended for ourselves when we needed you. Things did not make up for your time, but you gave me things, not time.

I no longer blame my parents. I understand they were working with what life experience they knew. I have learnt to accept and forgive my parents for what they didn`t know as parents; regarding the skills that I felt they needed to raise me, to protect and keep me safe.

"I will never leave you nor forsake you."

Hebrews 13:5 (NKJV)

CHAPTER 3

Pain

I know you misunderstood me, was it the way I looked?

Was it the way I walked?

Was it the way I sat?

Was it the way I spoke?

I asked myself why didn't I speak up, what was I afraid of?

You made me so angry when you didn`t accept me, or even when you didn`t ask me to explain what I was feeling, what was on my mind.

I really wanted to know what was on your mind.

I really wanted to know how you were feeling.

It felt like you didn`t want me to speak, and then I thought, "What are you hiding? What didn`t you want me to know?"

I felt angry that I was silent. I felt so angry with myself. Yes, I was angry with Pauline.

You would think I was happy because I had nice clothes, I had a nice home and family. Well, I wasn`t. I was hurting. My heart was broken. I didn`t have the language to describe my feelings. How could I know? I didn`t even know how to articulate my feelings.

Looking back now over my life I realise the person I was angry with was me. Yet I thought it was you; you who represent my parents; you who represent my family. You who represented my school. You didn`t explore what people like me were feeling. I could eventually hide behind working hard and serving at church. I hid behind my role as a mother and then as a grandmother.

But the time came when I knew something didn`t sit right with me. Becoming a Christian wasn`t enough to help me know who I was, I wasn`t applying the Word in all areas of my life. I was too emotional.

I loved to study, and going down the road of coaching helped me to put the icing on the cake. I could marry my roles together of Christian and coach, and the marriage worked.

I learnt to marry Pauline with Pauline-Elizabeth. Pauline was the old me and Pauline-Elizabeth the new me. The before, and now with Christ in my life.

The new mindset that I had was feeling good. It was like I was wearing a new set of garments. I felt comfortable, I was no longer behaving the way I was to myself. Yes, I was looking after my mind, I began to be calm. I could feel the calmness. I started to like myself. Do you know what it`s like to now like yourself, to respect and appreciate yourself?

Journey with me to age 18 while living in Jamaica when mummy and daddy were going through marital issues. Why didn`t I challenge what I saw and heard? Why did I spend years blaming myself and thinking that I should have spoken up and possibly that could have saved their marriage?

It wasn't my fault that my dad couldn't handle rejection and nearly took my mother's and my life.

It was a dark, quiet night and everyone was in bed. I had returned home to Jamaica from America and was exhausted partly from my journey, and also because I was helping in my mum's bar when I arrived. I had locked up and had gone to my bed where my mother was already asleep.

Whilst in America, I heard an inner voice saying to me to go back to Jamaica because "your dad is going to hurt your mum". It was strange hearing that voice, but I just knew I had to return. I had left to get away from my parents. I didn't want to be caught in the middle of their controversy anymore, but the voice was compelling and I knew I had to return.

I was in my bed, and my mum was sleeping beside me. I was woken by groans from mum. At first, I thought she was having a nightmare or hold-down. However, when I put my right arm out across her and tapped her calling out "Mum, mum!" my brother Chris rushed into the room.

It was not until then that we realised that mum and I had been attacked by my dad with a pitch fork.

I felt if he hadn't returned to England and walked away from his responsibility as husband and father, we would still be a happy family. Well, that's what I thought.

The hurtful thing is nobody explored the issues with me or us as a family. We received no counselling. Both my mother and I have physical scars. When this incident took place I didn't cry. The fact that we survived confirmed to me that there was a God, so I was grateful to be alive. It has been a long recovery from that day, and I am still recovering.

Why didn't I challenge, my dad? Why didn't I let him know that I was his little girl and felt deeply hurt by his action? I realised I was scared to speak up because I didn't want to hurt my mum. I was protecting her. Who was protecting me?

I allowed my dad to go to court, but I didn't want him to go to prison. I thought him being locked up and having to attend court was enough, but it was not because he never even acknowledged his action of almost taking my life, and as a little girl I thought I was his favourite because he never told me off. My mum was the strict one. I also thought I was saving my family from the shame, but people knew, the word went near and far.

... be transformed by the renewing of your mind,

Romans 12:2 (NKJV)

CHAPTER 4

Here I Am Screaming from
My Bright Colours

" **S**o, here I am wearing a striped jumper for school, coloured red, blue, green, yellow and black. The stripes run diagonally. It has a round neck neckline and it is three-quarter sleeves."

I wore it with a pleated navy-blue school skirt which I rolled up over my knees and wore white long socks with flat black shoes. I walked into school late as usual, because I didn`t wake up on time for school. I thought you would say, "You're late Pauline!" but you didn`t Miss.

I thought you would say, "Why aren`t you wearing your school shirt, tie and cardigan Pauline?" but you didn`t, did you Miss.

I thought you would call my mum to report me to her, but you didn`t Miss.

I wondered why you didn`t? I thought you would have called my mum who would tell me off, or at least that`s what I expected, so I could get you're her attention. "Why didn`t mummy realise that I was going to secondary school late, and not wearing the correct school uniform?

Oh yeah, it's because mummy you were busy working. You had a vision for the family to migrate to Jamaica."

Most West Indians who came to the UK in the early '50s had in mind that they were going to stay for only five years. Windrush generation

"You, like many women mummy, got married had children, and five years turned to seventeen years."

"Mummy I needed your attention. Miss, I needed some of your attention. I've got my hand raised, but it looks like no one could see me."

In my mind and my heart, my hand is raised.

"I am too scared to actually raise my hand and open my mouth and get your attention. So, here I am wearing my bright colours hoping you can read my mind."

"I remember mummy, I use to pray to God that I would talk in my sleep. So, you could know exactly what was on my mind. Looking back, I am glad it didn't happen, because I would have received the strap."

Jamaican's call it "a beating".

I loved, and to date, love wearing red garments. As a young woman, I was saying, "Keep off!"

I knew that red meant danger. So why was I wearing red the 'danger' colour but still needed my mummy and my teacher to notice me?

I never doubted your love for me mummy, I just felt you were too busy, and this left me time to overthink, I did very well. My emotions were all over the place, but I didn't know it. I just thought the best way to speak was through my colours.

*Arise, shine; For your light
has come!*

Isaiah 60:1 (NKJV)

CHAPTER 5

I Was Hiding

"*Y*ou might be asking who was I hiding from? Let me tell you, it might shock you."

"I was hiding from me. Yes, I said it, I was hiding from me. Remember I didn't know I had low self–esteem."

I needed to know who I was. And I started to see myself as two people. Pauline is my birth name. Elizabeth my spiritual name. I sensed the Lord speaking to me, saying Elizabeth is my new name because when excited to do his will and I connect with like-minded people there is a leaping feeling I experience. Just as when "Elizabeth heard the salutation of Mary, the babe leaped in her womb". Luke 1: 41. Sharing my story by writing my book is allowing me to Own my Voice, my baby is leaping.

I had to learn, as I said before to marry Pauline and Pauline-Elizabeth. I truly believe I was scared to know who I was and what I could achieve in life. I began to see that I had been lying to myself. You see, I was saying one thing, while my heart was saying something else, there was no action to manifest what I wanted which was a relationship with my mum, and the liberty to speak my truth to help others own their voice. Knowing that there may be consequences. I had regularly quoted "I am fearfully and wonderfully made" Psalm 139:14, yet I wasn`t stepping out in faith to approach my mum so we could talk about our past. I also needed to launch my coaching business. I was telling myself, mummy is not going to acknowledge my pain, and I won`t remember what to say to my audience.

I said to myself, "I have the mind of Christ."

Let this mind be in you, which was also in Christ Jesus" Philippians 2:5

Yet for years I had felt fear, and could not shift it, and no one realised.

I thank God I no longer feel the fear. In 2018 while on holiday I was able to speak to my mum about some of the things that troubled me for years. On Wednesday 24th July 2021 I launched out into the deep and started my Women Empowerment coaching session, "Own your voice" via zoom. There is no turning back for me now, the only person that could stop me is me, and I am no longer hiding from myself.

At first, I was scared to ask people for help. I didn`t want people to know what I didn`t know.

"So, yes, I was ashamed, I believed for my age I should have more; but who said I should have more?"

Nobody was criticizing me. You are right, I was criticizing myself.

I thought I wasn`t enough, I thought I didn`t have enough. So, how could I expect to have what I want if I didn`t ask for help? I looked the part, I talked the talk, but I wasn`t walking the walk. I didn`t want to talk because I was ashamed, I thought people would say I should know better.

I didn't know how to stretch myself, I lived in my comfort zone. However, I knew I needed to be in my stretch zone, but I was scared.

I am so grateful the day I stumbled on coaching, it made me start to value myself. I started speaking up a little. My hand was halfway up. So, I knew I was trying.

I believe some of you may have been there when everyone thinks you have got it all together, and you know that's not the truth.

Well, what topped it for me is when I started to love myself and be grateful for life instead of looking at what I didn't have. I was appreciating what I did have. I was experiencing a mind shift.

My shyness was going, I started to acknowledge the work I was doing on myself. I was now owning my voice. I liked how I sounded. I didn't care what others were saying about me; it wasn't important. What was important, is what Pauline-Elizabeth was saying to and about Pauline-Elizabeth.

... *"Be strong and coura-geous. Do not be afraid; do not be discouraged, for the Lord your God will be with you wherever you go."*

Joshua 1:9

CHAPTER 6

Please Ask Me How I Am Feeling

I am hurting I am a 12-year-old pre-teenager, what do I know about feelings. I don't even know if I am hurting from my head or my heart. "All I know is you hurt me. You hurt me by not being there with me. I know you had to work but I needed you. I was a little girl who was always around big people, especially males. My hair styles were that of a big woman, but I was only 12 years old. I needed you to ask me how I was feeling."

There I was 'seen and not heard', wearing my bright colours, but afraid to open my mouth.

Looking back now, it was as if I was wearing a mask. I could be in the crowd at school during lunchtime. We had dance competitions. Oh, how I looked forward to lunchtime. I would dance and win the dance competitions. There, I could express my feelings through my dance.

"Did anyone ask me, how I felt after dancing? No!"

"I so wanted a big hug, but you were so busy working." You were some-one I always admired, because you were a role model, as wife and mother. I saw you as a strong woman who came to the UK intending to be a Nurse, and you achieved it. You are resilient, focused, independent, determined, resourceful, and very good at organising yourself and the family. You are wise with money and you know how to save. Owning two homes was a big achievement for me to observe. You were not afraid to work. You did your full-time nursing job and an extra evening job. Even my friends admired you because you were always well dressed, and you looked young and trendy. Everyone saw you as a lady, someone to admire. You made sure I didn't lack any material things.

I remember trying to smoke at the age of 12, I would be upstairs on the bus coming home from a church activity or hiding in the bathroom looking in the mirror. Mummy wasn't a smoker likewise my aunty Barbara. You were both hard-working wives and mothers. I couldn't smoke because it would not meet the high standards you had modelled for me. Thank you both for being role models.

Your busy working life meant that you couldn't be at home with me and my brothers Christopher and Tony, so Daddy did some of the housework because he was not prepared to do a second job. "The devil finds work for idle hands" is a proverb I grew up hearing. I became curious after listening to a school friend at secondary school talk about her relationship with her boyfriend. I desired to have a boyfriend. I am so sorry. Looking back at the age of 12, I had no business with a boyfriend.

"Mummy I didn't hear you express your love. I needed to hear, "I love you, Paul. Well done Paul." I needed your hugs, but you were busy. I remember the times when you took me to the cinema when you were a first aider, but you were working. So, I sat alone watching the movie. I did enjoy the Tootie Fruity ice cream and the 'Carry on' movies, but I still felt alone.

"Before I formed you in the womb I knew you; Before you were born I sanctified you;

...

Jeremiah 1:5 (NKJV)

CHAPTER 7

Will Somebody Feel My Pain

*M*y little heart was broken, that's how it felt.

"I can see my heart in two pieces and I wanted you to see it too."

It felt like my heart was dropped on the floor and shattered in pieces, at times. It was in so many pieces, it felt like it could never be put back together again. Just like Humpty Dumpty who fell off the wall.

"I needed you to be able to look at my heart and help me put it back together again, but you were *too* busy working to notice."

"I needed you to be able to feel my pain, of course, I came from you. You should be able to feel my pain. You felt me when I was in your womb. It feels like you are hurting me. So now it's time to hurt you, so here I go." I talked about you to my friends, I talked about you to family members, and no one said that I shouldn't. I liked how talking about you made me feel because it made me feel they were on my side. It made me feel they understood or cared.

I hurt you with my words, I hurt you with my behaviour. I thought it felt good. There I was, this vexed, angry, push-up mouth teenager who couldn`t wait to be 16. I thought that was when I could do what I want to do. This angry behaviour went on into my adult life.

As a teenager, you wouldn`t hear me so now as an adult you are going to hear me. So, I am no longer speaking out of my bright colours, even though I still wear them, especially red. I was speaking out of my anger, and my voice would raise, as I felt that was the only way you would hear me

I felt you hurt me with your words because I heard the things you said about me to family and friends in my adult life. You really hurt me with your words. I thought, "You don`t love me."

What hurt also was you didn`t look at my school work. You didn`t know my academic level and didn't show any interest in finding out how I was doing. I was scared of doing Maths. You let Tony teach Chris and me during the first two weeks of the summer holidays, but he wasn`t able to teach me at that level, and two weeks could not have met my shortfall or filled in my gaps. The sad thing is you didn't even realise how far behind I was with Maths. Somehow I got through life without having sat my Maths Secondary School Education Certificate. English, I loved so it`s no surprise that I am writing this book.

You didn`t say let`s go out and have some mother and daughter time. Oh, how I longed to spend time with you as a little girl.

Why didn`t I just say that mummy, "Can we have a girl's night out?" Oh yeah, 'children are seen and not heard', I knew that very well. I didn`t know how to express my needs in words. I expected you to read my mind mummy." Reflecting on wanting to talk in my sleep as a teenager, I am so glad God did not give me that desire. Because I understand now that God can give us the desires of our heart. (Psalm 37:4) I believe we should be mindful about what we pray or ask for in life. Looking back now, it was my duty to cover my mum`s shame, but I was so bitter, all I wanted to do was expose her. Little did I know I was reacting and talking out of my pain. There were times when I said, "I believe I was rejected from the womb." I wondered if the pregnancy was traumatic, but I didn't want to ask. Your generation was so secretive.

Not having the confidence to speak up by asking you questions about your life broke my heart, and caused me so much pain, and made me bitter.

I choose to speculate that you and my dad, had marital issues but were very good at masking them. My brothers and I didn't see or hear anything, and if they did, they didn't say.

Residing in Jamaica and UK you were the main breadwinner. Sometimes it felt like you wore the pants in the home. If I asked daddy for some money he always said "Ask your mum, I gave her all the money." If I wanted to go out and you were at work, daddy would say, "Go before your mother come." Now that I can reflect on it, I can see that you did not work as a team with regards to how I was parented.

For years I struggled to understand mummy, after all, we went through nearly losing our lives when daddy attacked us, how Mr Dyer and Mr Williams got priority over my brothers and me.

I remember when you became unwell and I was asking Mr Williams to take you to the doctor, he ignored me. I thank God that Brother Lambert came along and noticed that the shutters for the shop were still down on a Saturday, you hadn't become a Christian as yet. He saw you looked unwell and told Mr Williams that you need to see a doctor. I was not allowed to go. I felt so rejected as your daughter and then began to feel that it was my fault that you were unwell. You had suffered from a mild heart attack.

This hurt me for years, it made me withdraw, I became fearful to even attempt to challenge you, should anything happen to you, I would see it as my fault.

I didn't feel comfortable in Jamaica, yet I loved the country, I used the opportunity of my two pregnancies to return to the UK.

Deep down, I knew that Mr Williams was not the right person to look up to as a stepfather. I was grateful to God when the day arose when he was no longer in your life.

It took several years before you became a Christian, and even though I was a Christian I was still bitter because our relationship was still broken. Like a little girl I was yearning for a restoration to take place with us. Yet I didn't know this would happen.

You visited the UK several times and didn't stay with me, I was so hurt. Now that we are on good terms, I am no longer looking for certain answers to yesterday, I am grateful that you are alive and I was able to forgive myself, forgive you, and hear you ask me to forgive you. I look forward to my long holidays in Jamaica. It's my grandchildren that keep me in the UK. My children understand my passion to spend more time in the country that I fell in love with at the age of 15.

The blessing of the Lord makes one rich, And He adds no sorrow with it.

Proverbs 10:22 (NKJV)

CHAPTER 8

A journey to change?

"*I*can't stay here, it hurts too much. When you wanted me to go to Jamaica at the age of 15, I said no. Who was I to say no? Well, I was a stroppy teenager who had friends in the UK. Childhood friends like Sonia Wynter, Yvonne Wynter and Carol Pettigrew. I didn't want to leave them.

Even though I was sad, Sonia, Yvonne and Carol didn't know it, but that was okay because we had a lot in common. We liked to dance, and that is how I was able to mask my pain. I just danced. Oh, how I loved to dance.

I was hurting. I was the girl with two brothers. I wished I had a big sister to talk to. Perhaps I would have felt less lonely.

I remember my inner voice saying to me "Go to Jamaica you won't have any friends, but you won't get any more beating." Why was I getting beaten?

I loved going to the youth clubs, so I could dance, but my mum didn't approve. The thing is, she didn't say why.

That would have helped mummy if you had said why I shouldn't go. All I wanted to do was dance, I was able to speak through my dancing.

Looking back, I was speaking to myself. When I danced, I expressed with my hands and with my body movement. I could smile and be sad without opening my mouth because I believed I had no voice.

Migrating to Jamaica I believed would stop the beatings but I didn't like the thought of not having friends. Every time I came in from the youth club, which I had sneaked out to attend. I would hear, "Put your night clothes on Paul" and that's when I got the beatings.

Now it is seen as child abuse.

It was so strange, I hated getting the beatings but I still went to the youth clubs, or other places, that I lied about, so I could attend. Sonia, Yvonne and Carol didn't have to lie to their parent's, plus Sonia and Yvonne had an older sister, Audrey who would always come to my rescue. My parents would trust her to look after me.

I suppose the beatings was the only way of getting your attention mummy. You didn't sit me down and talk to me.

I wanted to hurt you, and I suppose you were hurting because of my behaviour. I was thirteen and promiscuous.

So, I agreed to go to Jamaica.

Of course, I had no choice, but now I was going willingly. I thought maybe you will start hearing me in Jamaica. Maybe you will start loving me in Jamaica."

"The Spirit of the Lord God is upon Me, Because the Lord has anointed Me …

Isaiah 61:1 (NKJV)

CHAPTER 9

Restoration and healing

I decided that I am coming out of hiding. However, no one could let me out, because no one locked me up. I was looking for someone to rescue me, but rescue me from what? Rescue me from who? Let me answer my question.

"I wanted you to rescue me, mummy. As a little girl and young woman, I depended on you mummy to think for me. I didn`t know how to think for myself. I would ask your opinion on what to wear. In my early 30`s I remember asking you what questions to ask my boyfriend. How naive I was. Mummy, I remember that I saw you as my God. I even told you that, and you said "Then you were stupid then, weren`t you."

Oh, how those words hurt me. It felt like the words cut me deeply. Looking back, you were right, how could you be my God?

As a Christian, I now understand that "For thou shalt worship no other god: for the Lord, whose name is Jealous, is a jealous God" Exodus 34: 14

I needed to learn how to rescue myself, from the deep dark pit that I was in. That place of loneliness, of wanting my mum, that no one was aware of. I am grateful for my daughter Tasha and son Selvin who allowed me to be on the journey towards becoming who God destined me to be. At times Tasha stepped in and her brother was not happy because she was in my mother role, as I was too busy with working and my church duties. Do you see how history repeats itself? Of course, there were things they needed to know about the family that I was not disclosing. I didn't know how to tell my son that I nearly lost my life. I just allowed him for years to think that I was a naughty girl. I could not explain to him how I got the scars on my right arm. I could not tell him that the scars were there as a result of my dad almost taking my life at age 18. How was he to deal with that sorry truth?

It wasn't until I stumbled on coaching in my late 50's that I started to become strong. I started to develop inner strength, and as years went on, I began to see how I had failed myself. Yes. I had failed Pauline-Elizabeth. I am my rescuer, with the guidance of God.

Yes, I still loved wearing bright colours, and I was beginning to speak up, but I was still shy. The real me was still wearing a mask. I didn't ask questions, I didn't challenge people's actions, and if I did question things in my adult life, I believed my motive for asking the question, was misunderstood or misinterpreted.

I didn't have wisdom in the early stage of my Christian life, so I suppose that is why my motive could have been questioned. I also remember, I spoke very fast. I was a very angry woman.

As I started to listen to Coaches, I started to add value to myself. People like Les Brown, Lisa Nichols, Iyanla Vanzant, Mel Robbins and Andy Harrington helped to reshape my thinking. I started to recognise the lies I had told myself, about myself.

I told myself that "I wasn't enough. I didn't have enough. I wasn't good enough".

What a big fat lie! I had listened to my negative chatter and believed it. I learnt to change my story "I am more than enough. I have enough. I am good enough."

I started to say affirmation`s and do visualizations. I was now hearing myself. I could feel myself. I could see myself, and I was beginning to like the new me. I got brave and did Facebook lives. I knew that I was in a new place and I was loving myself.

I practised self-care, and I was experiencing self-love. I looked in the mirror every day and I was able to say "You look good Pauline-Elizabeth"

I kept saying affirmations to myself until I believed what I was saying to myself. Oh, how I was loving the new me, I realised people could only hurt me emotionally if I allowed them. It was my job to protect my heart.

I was sounding different. I was liking the sound of my voice. I no longer cared what people said about me. I knew what they said was none of my business. What mattered was what I said to myself about myself. I knew that "I can do all things through Christ which strengtheneth me" (Philippians 4:13 NKJV) was not just a scripture passage that I quoted as a Christian; I was owning it.

I started to encourage people to be the best version of themselves, own their voice, and be their own rescue. While learning to forgive and love themselves.

This is what was working for me. The more I became one with myself and forgave myself, it made it easier for me to forgive and love the people that hurt me.

I began to see my pain turn to pleasure. My relationship with my mum was going through restoration. I was able to ask for her forgiveness, and she was able to ask me to forgive her. My mum started to speak her truth to me. I was freely able to speak my truth to her, without holding back. My mum had taken the mask off. WOW!

I am so grateful for our healing, I know that some of you reading fully understand the weight I was carrying, and the relief I am now feeling. For my readers who never got the opportunity to say sorry or hear sorry, from their loved ones. It is okay. I encourage you to do the self-work, it's not too late for you. You can receive that peace, and self-relief.

Being able to write this book is a dream come true. Mummy, we were both in pain and needed to count it all joy, our pain has turned into pleasure. We can talk and laugh about them now. I choose to say I needed my pain to help shape me. What I thought was breaking me, was MAKING me a better person.

I choose to see my husband as a good friend. I have come to accept that "absence didn't make the heart grow fonder". Absence enabled me to put self-worth and value to myself. We were two broken people, that were hurting each other. We had different goals, which should have been explored before we said yes to marriage. Being the person I am, I wanted to help my husband. I didn't realise the emotional cost that would be involved. I loved and will always love him, however, I didn't know that I didn't love Pauline-Elizabeth.

I accept that Selvin Senior will always be a part of my life. He is the father of my son and grandfather to my five grandchildren. I just will not be his wife. I grew up hearing "a good friend is better than pocket money" so I thank you, my friend. I see you as a gift. Selvyn, you came as a gift that enabled me to understand life. And how important it is to have an attitude of GRATITUDE. When people come into our lives, it is important to acknowledge what we have learnt, they came to serve us. We need to be looking for the good, but sadly we see the bad.

The best thing with the future is that it comes one day at a time.

By Abraham Lincoln[2]

---

[2] Schulich Leader Scholarship, Lerebours, Roose Clifford (Fall 2013) "The best thing about the future is that it comes one day at a time", Internet cited 13.12.2021 at: https://www. schulichleaders.com/best-thing-about-future-it-comes-one-day-time

CHAPTER 10

Two broken hearts

*H*ow did I get it so wrong? I wanted someone to love me, yet I was not ready to be loved. I didn`t even know what love was.

I remember when I decided to return to a relationship with my son`s dad and go down the road of marriage. I felt it was safe because I knew him since I was seventeen years old. I thought I had been out with him twice before; I know him, we know each other`s family, what possibly could go wrong. He had been married, so there must be something for me to learn. Considering I had never been married before or lived with a man.

I was an independent woman in my 50`s who raised my 2 children on my own. Looking back over my life, it felt like I had some kind of covering over me. I wasn`t attracted to just any men. My son`s dad was a fashion designer and that is what attracted him to me. I was studying Fashion Design at college in Jamaica. Remember I love clothes.

To be honest the men that I did find attractive were married or in a relationship. They were my friends, I was just happy to have them in my life. (If you are reading my book, you know who you are, you always told me not to worry things will be alright with mummy and me. I really appreciate you and value your friendship. People wouldn`t understand our friendship, you encouraged me, danced with me, you romanced me. You laughed with me, and I am sure you cried with me. Thank you for your love, but you couldn`t be with me. Now I understand the Lord was protecting me. He was the one covering me, keeping me safe all these years. He knew my heart. He knew I needed to be loved but the love I needed was His "unconditional love". God accepted me as me. I am so grateful God didn`t tell anyone my fault`s. "He looked beyond my faults and saw my needs" (Ramboo, Dottie, (2003) "He looked beyond my faults" New Spring Publishing, Inc. It is clear God wanted me to learn how to first love Pauline-Elizabeth, then I would be better equipped to give and receive love. I needed to know my self-worth. I sensed the Lord saying when I got married, that I had prepared my heart.

My hardened heart for my son's dad was softening. I had been betrayed by his unfaithfulness. I had been neglected whilst I was pregnant, physically and emotionally. I left to get support back in the UK and he showed no care, not even at Christmas had he cared about me as I carried his child. I made my mind up to support myself, and that is what I did. I returned to my friend Yvette who supported me. I had said I would never go back to him, now here I was returning to him for the third time.

Looking back, my mind on the other hand was far from being prepared for marriage. I was not prepared for what would come in the rela-tionship, especially how I would respond to the pressure that came when I became redundant from working in the Residential Children`s home. I didn't get the support I felt I needed from my husband, and I was not giving him the support he needed from me.

I had sent for him from Jamaica. We got married on Valentine's week-end 2010 in Jamaica, he arrived in the UK in June of the same year, and by the end of the year the children`s home was closing down.

He did not have a full-time job and was not entitled to public resources for another two years. When he had arrived, I had prayed for the Lord to restore his passion for Fashion Designing, and this happened. When I met Selvyn he was a Fashion Designer and I was studying Fashion. I was on my way home from Duffs Business College waiting at the bus stop at Cross Roads in Kingston. His brother Chevens who I knew first had offered to give me a lift home. Learning that Selvyn was a Fashion Designer and seeing the way he dressed I instantly fell for him. I felt that he could teach me about the fashion industry.

Being married to him and seeing the reality of my prayers come through, I admired his dedication to designing, pattern-making and sewing. Everything he did was done with care and attention. His sewing was exquisite. He would stay up all night to sew, then deliver the garment to the people that ordered it, but then the money was his. He did not think of my needs. He was then freely able to buy his white rum which he secretly consumed. He did not consider helping me. For me paying the bills was the priority. I remember when he got Right to Remain in the UK, I received £40 as he was now able to access public funds. I did not disclose this to him. I was happy for the extra money to help pay the bills. I knew that unlike Jamaica "If rain-wet you the sun won`t dry you." I felt he is earning from his sewing. When he became aware of the stipend I received, he was very angry. This caused him to distrust me, and he saw me as a thief. I also realised that I was not showing to him the respect that he expected. We were not good at communicating with each other. I felt he did not understand that God was blessing him to sew so he could step up and be the breadwinner of our home. I wanted to honour and support him. I put clients his way, and these friends of mine wanted to help, but alas, as his business grew, and I supported him to grow the business, things did not improve. He did not want my support and he did not feel he needed to support me.

I was also happy to marry him because we knew each other's families and I also had a son for him, I felt, "better the devil you know than the one you don't know", not that he was a devil. He had been married before, got several kids so he must be able to teach me a lot about family life. Well, that's what I thought.

I love the song "Little is much when God is in it" sung by Gaither vocal band, written by Kreiger Conrad / Kreiger Donna / Suffield, Mrs F W, I wanted us to work at our relationship. It was hard for me as my mum did not approve of me getting married to Selvyn, as he was unemployed and everyone knew he was a drinker. As a young woman, my mum said, "Don't marry a poor man." I thought once you love each other you can work at making a life together. Clearly, mummy knew what she was saying, as my dad didn't make life easy for her. I loved Selvyn and believed he loved me, but the financial strain came unexpectedly and neither of us was prepared for this. My priority was keeping a roof over our heads, whereas he thought if I wasn't working I don't have to pay a mortgage. So, I was struggling with the misinformed information he was receiving from his newfound friends. These people did not mean us well. I then developed a distrust of him. I felt he did not value the marriage enough to work with me to ensure we got back on our feet. I had raised two adult children on my own. I believed I had a good track record of knowing how to survive in the UK. I knew how to tighten my belt, how to make ends meet. I thought in the situation we were in that 'two heads are better than one'. I sensed he allowed fear to overwhelm him. He could also tell I was pulling away from him, as I could not depend on him emotionally, or financially.

I recall saying to Selvyn, my husband, that the day is going to come when I will not be wasting my time talking about the same thing over and over. I will refrain from talking, because I have had enough, and that is exactly what eventually happened I wanted out of the marriage.

I am a woman of faith, I knew God would bring me through. I wanted God to bring us through, but he was more looking to leave. He said, "The same way you have your home you don`t I think I want one too." I thought that`s a strange thing to say, that`s not how married couples live. So as my mum would say "You take sleep and mark death" which means I was watching his every move. Then I learnt from him that he and his ex-wife didn`t always live together, so he was used to living alone, doing things his way. Interestingly, so was I.

There were times I would go and stay with either of my children when I just didn`t want to go home. He was good at cooking so that was not an issue for him. That was one of the qualities that attracted me to him, he would cook for me. When he came to the UK I was working and when I came home my meal was ready and when I took my meals to work I felt special. I must admit I didn`t make it easy for my husband, as I saw red flags early in our marriage. I was unable to trust him with my heart, and he did not trust me fully either.

The bible states "Do not yoke yourself with unbelievers" (2 Corinthians 6:14 NIV) When we were preparing for marriage, he was willing to become a Christian or so I believed. He attended church with me in Jamaica and even in the UK. Once he started his sewing he no longer attended church. I realised I only held onto 1 part of the above scripture which was "unbeliever". I said he was not an unbeliever, because he believes there is a God. He was not prepared to accept the Lord as his personal saviour. For me, this was bringing a strain on our relationship which was rocky before he had even left Jamaica.

My dear readers, I need you to see my heart which was in two pieces, well that is how it felt, one of my wedding songs was "Two hearts that beat as one". However, it was two broken hearts, that could never beat as one. Before I could know my husband, I needed to know Pauline-Elizabeth.

Selvyn`s heart was broken from his past life in Jamaica, and mine was broken from my past yearning for love and attention. White rum was his comfort and going to church was mine. I made it clear he had a choice, me or the white rum. Struggling to fit into the UK, the white rum won. I had to release him and release myself, so I could fall in love with Pauline-Elizabeth.

When I told him that I dance until 1.00 am, or on special occasions 3.00 am on the Caribbean Social Forum Zoom during the Lockdown, he was convinced that I had found myself a new man. I was pleased to say I had fallen in love with myself.

I had stumbled on Coaching with The Coaching Academy when Selvyn left and I enrolled on a course, it enabled me to do some self-care work, and I realised that I didn`t love myself. WOW what a surprise, I started working on my self-esteem. And I knew there was no going back to Selvyn, we had broken up five times. Who does that? Well, I did and I could not walk away. He was happy to attend the Anglican church and I was a Pentecostal. I kept saying we don`t speak the same language. He didn`t have the finance so he was drinking it was discreetly. "Well, a leopard never changes his spots" I do believe people can change, they need a good enough reason to make change happen. Selvyn would always say "me no kiah" which means he doesn`t care, he would always say "au so me tan" meaning that's how I am. Well, I had been a Christian long enough and did enough self-care work, to understand that I can only change myself. So, I said, "Hit the road Jack".

... "The things which are impossible with men are possible with God."

Luke 18:27 (NKJV)

CHAPTER 11

Face to Face With Reality

I was too angry. I was trying to express my thoughts, looking back now, I made you angry mummy. Oh, how I thank God for wisdom, and God is my teacher. I am grateful for my friend Mary Abrahams, who taught me how to love my family, even when I didn't want to.

Mary, you reminded me that the bible says, "Honour thy father and thy mother: that thy days may be long upon the land which the Lord thy God giveth thee." (Exodus 20:12)

I needed my days to be long, so I could fulfil the desires of my heart. And clearly, I had not been honouring my parent`s, because I was angry and bitter. Regarding what I thought they should have done especially when my brother Tony died. I did not feel supported with organising his burial. It was as if my son had died and it was my responsibility to bury him.

I knew I had to consult God in prayer, to change me; to break down my stony heart; to take away the bitterness and hurt I was nursing, especially towards you mummy.

Here goes God again. He used my dear friend Donna. Donna, you looking after your mum was of great help in my healing journey. I know your mum wasn't always nice to you, and when you became a Seventh-day Adventist Christian, I saw God melt your heart to love and serve your mum. Forgiveness came easy for you, thank you, my friend. Thank you, Sister Mary. Your mother wasn't always nice to you but you still loved her; you had a forgiving heart. God used you and Donna, so I had no way of escaping.

The negative chatter and distorted vision I had was that my mum didn't love me. I was hurting, it was like the little girl who was yearning for her mummy, I was a little girl in a big woman's body, I had not fully grown up.

Then the Lord used my aunty Ena to minister to my mummy, she is my mum's little sister. My aunt is also a Seventh-day Adventist Christian. My mum's heart started to soften. I knew it was the teaching mum was receiving, as the Adventist church teaching focuses on the family.

All my complaining of why no one couldn't hear me was okay; God was hearing me. The time came when God directed me to go to Jamaica for six weeks to serve my mum. I struggled to plan that trip. So off I went. My mum was preparing for me, but the preparation included if I said anything that she was not happy with she was ready to answer me. Clearly, the answer was not going to be what I expected, it was going to hurt me, but God had a plan. He knew my heart. He knew I wanted to make it right with my mum. He used the preaching at the Seventh-day Adventist church to be what mummy and I needed to hear and since 2018 I am pleased to say my mum and me are experiencing restoration in our relationship.

I now understand your pain mummy, I know you did the best you could with what you knew at the time. After talking with you I can see your role as wife and mother was not an easy task. Mummy thank you for sharing your truth, I am now learning as a mother and grandmother not to hurt with my words. I am learning to be patient with myself and to forgive myself and others. Jesus said, "Forgive them they know not what they do."

I remember when I became a Christian in September 1992, my mum said to my aunt Ena that she could not remember what I looked like. She couldn't see my face in her mind's eye. I thank God that he was transforming me, and my mum could sense that happening.

... My grace is sufficient for you, for My strength is made perfect in weakness."

. . .

2 Corinthians 12:9 (NKJV)

CHAPTER 12

I Am Screaming

"*H*i am over here, can`t you see me? I don`t think you can miss me. I am the one wearing bright colours, especially red. I know red say`s "keep off!" I grew up hearing red is the colour of danger, and is the colour of the stoplight. By wearing red, I thought I was extending my hand to say "Keep your distance!" This is how I saw my actions in my mind. At the same time in my heart, I want to talk to you. I want to tell you what`s on my mind. I want to tell you what`s in my heart. I want to give you a piece of my mind. Here I am! I want to talk." "Look over here I am the one dancing, I love dancing, I can`t stop. Even if I am dancing on my own, I still enjoy it."

"Why am I dancing? I am trying to get your attention. I need you to speak to me, I don`t know how to speak to you. So please start the conversation. Ask me something, please ask me anything?"

"Okay, since you won`t ask me anything, can I speak now?" Here I go. "Hold on, you don`t seem to be listening. What am I doing wrong?"

I was standing right in front of you. I am in the room, for some strange reason my voice doesn`t seem to matter. I was standing right next to you. I know you didn't say it out loud, but that's how I felt, and I felt invisible.

I came across Franklin, Anderson J, (2004) *From Brotherhood to Manhood: How Black men Rescue Their Relationships and Dreams from the Invisibility Syndrome*, Published by Turner Publishing, New York. The author talks about the feeling people get when their abilities, personality and worth are disregarded. I thought that sounds like me.

I am struggling with 'Invisibility Syndrome'. I am wearing these bright colours for nothing. I know it won't always be like this. However, I feel like the black sheep in the family. I know you didn't say it but that's how I felt. Why was I excluded from the family parties? What did I do wrong? I really wanted to know. Now I understand I didn't do anything wrong, and you were not ignoring me. This was my opportunity to G.R.O.W, Go – Reach – Own -Win. (Pat Reid Mentor of ICAN Community Church, Entrepreneurs Support Group quoted this I needed to find myself. Owning my voice, enabled me to find myself. Thank you for giving me the space to G.R.O.W. I am a better Christian, Mother, Daughter, and Friend. I have been able to reset my life; I pushed the reset button, and there is no returning to my old self, for me.

... I am the voice of one cry-ing in the wilderness ...

John 1:23 KJV

CHAPTER 13

Don`t Tell Me to Shut Up

I have been listening to you for years, I didn`t block you from speaking. Each time I opened my mouth you contradicted me. It felt like, my views were not valid, I started to doubt myself. I felt that my input was not appreciated. I didn`t challenge you.

Then I realised I couldn`t shut up, what I was saying is what others were thinking. So now I am speaking for all of us. You know who you are. I don't need to mention your name. I am speaking my truth, which may also be a part of your truth.

For there to be a change in any area of life, someone`s voice has to be heard. So, let it be my voice. I held myself back because I was scared, I thought "If I speak my truth it would hurt you, but by not speaking my truth, I was hurting myself."

It`s my story. I needed to experience freedom. How nice it feels to be free, to be free from me. To be able to look me in the mirror and say, "It`s okay Pauline-Elizabeth. The cage door is open; you don`t have to go back inside."

I have a platform for you to express yourself, and once you experience that freedom, teach others to do the same. I gave you R.O.O.T.S (Restoration of our Troubled Soul) Prayer Ministry. You didn't even realise what I was doing with you, in you and through you. You just trusted me." These are the words I sensed the Lord saying to me while I wrote this chapter.

I am now free to be Pauline-Elizabeth on the 'A Voice Crying in the Wilderness' platform each month on a Sunday evening. Women are encouraged to share and hear stories, own their voice while standing in their truth, and become the best version of themselves. "WOW! WOW! WOW! You are getting there Pauline-Elizabeth. I am really proud of you." is what I would say to myself.

I grew up hearing "Self-praise is no recommendation" and "Don't blow your own trumpet". I had to learn to encourage myself. I wasn't waiting on people anymore, I had to speak to me, and it worked.

One thing I know, and that is I have always trusted the Lord. The person I didn't trust was Pauline-Elizabeth. So, I am no longer afraid to say no. I won't shut up; "It's my season. It's my turn. It's my time" is what my spiritual Mother Bishop Vivienne Downes would always say to me.

Tapping into Personal Performance Coaching, was the vehicle that transported me on a new life journey. I knew this was my way to help people especially women get from pain to pleasure, I knew I had something special and I couldn't keep it to myself. My faith was taking me in a new direction, I was no longer limited to the church building. What God was doing would enable me to touch lives near and far.

Now I pushed the boat out even further by enrolling in the Public Speaker University with Andy Harrington, it's too late to turn back now. I know my payoff for investing in myself is self-full-filling, this is definitely a big win.

Hear, O Lord, when I cry with my voice: have mercy also upon me, and answer me.

Psalms 27:7 (KJV)

CHAPTER 14

It's My Voice

I have found my voice. Hello, I have found my voice. The question is, was my voice lost, and if it was lost, how was it lost? Let me answer my question. It's as if I had tucked it in a box and put the lid on it and forgot where I had put the box. Even if had found it, I didn't have the key because I had lost that too."

WOW! WOW! WOW! I'm feeling happy! I had been singing "I'm locked up; they won't let me out!" This is a song my son Selvin Junior sang as a teenager when I put him on curfew for his behaviour.

"Can somebody pinch me, please? The bird has flown never to return. I have found Pauline-Elizabeth; it feels so good. Where have you been all my life Pauline-Elizabeth? Do you have any idea how much I missed you? Do you have any idea how much I wanted to speak to you Pauline-Elizabeth? I am glad God alone knows my thoughts." Knowing my self-worth, and accepting that I had low self-esteem all these years is a light bulb experience. I had been told that to look in the mirror is vanity, so I didn't look too much at myself. As a result, I didn't fully look at myself because I didn't think it was right to do so. Now I know, whatever people say or think about me, is none of my business. I always knew that God loves me, but to be able to accept that it's okay to love myself has me in awe. I can't stop looking in the mirror, each time I say "Hello beautiful!" When I hear myself, I believe it! I feel good about myself.

So now that I have found you, voice, I don't ever want to lose you. I will say what you tell me to say. If I feel scared, I will just look in the mirror, because that's where I see you. When I feel sad, I can look at you and be encouraged by you. You will affirm and remind me of who I am; a child of God. "For I am fearfully and wonderfully made: marvellous are thy works; and my soul knoweth right well". Psalms 139:14 You understand me, you are not afraid to say, "I love you Pauline-Elizabeth". You put words in my mouth."

"Thank you for being patient with me Pauline-Elizabeth. I didn't understand who I was, I didn't understand the real power of my voice. I always quoted "Death and life are in the power of the tongue: ..." Proverb 18: 21"

I looked confident, but I was scared to open my mouth and speak my truth. I didn't want people to know what I felt I should know as a mother and grandmother, now at age 63 I am not afraid to ask for help, I can be vulnerable, knowing that's where my strength is.

And we know that all things work together for good to them that love God, to them who are the called according to his purpose.

Romans 8:28 (KJV)

CHAPTER 15

I Will Live My Truth

I am a Voice Crying in the Wilderness. My voice is so distinct. I remember when I didn`t like my voice. Now I love my voice; my voice is my tool.

"And the Lord said unto him, what is that in thine hand? And he said, A rod" *Exodus 4:2*

Moses, who was slow in speech, at the Lord's request threw down the rod and it transformed into a snake.

I remember asking the Lord what did I have and heard "Your big mouth." I thought, "Ouch". Yes, that was painful to hear because I knew I had not used wisdom in the early days when I had painful life experiences. When people had hurt me and I tried to express myself but did not do a good job at it.

So now I am telling myself that I am here to stay, and I am telling you. I know some of you will not be able to handle my brightness, so please "put on sunglasses" as Lisa Nichols my virtual Transformational Coach would say. I say, "Just look away."

I have found Pauline-Elizabeth and I actually like her. In fact, I have come to love her. I can`t continue this journey without her.

On several occasions, Pauline wants to rise and behave in a fashion that reflects her pain. I have to tell her, "Shut up! I don`t want to hear your negative chatter. I want to hear what Pauline-Elizabeth has to say. Pauline-Elizabeth speaks from a place of pleasure, peace, calm, love and joy." I can now find pleasure in my pain. Yes! You heard me right. I was feeling a bit low in spirit, and when I had a Coaching session my coach Sadef asked, "How would you like the session to flow today?"

I said, "Just give me an exercise."

Sedef had me look at my life in five stages, from ages 0-63 broken into five stages. When I looked at my life from 0-14, I saw pain.

I closed my eyes while speaking about my life. What felt painful Sadef taught me to use my right hand and push aside, with an attitude of "I will deal with you later. Right now I need to hear myself talk".

When I finished talking about my pain, Sadef asked me to identify the gift.

I said, "Gift? Is there a gift in my pain?" As I reflected on my pain I heard, "Gratitude!"

I was grateful to be alive. I remember at age 13 when my parent`s decided that I can`t have a boyfriend, I almost took my own life. Gratitude is the appropriate gift to me.

Now Pauline-Elizabeth can live her truth. I can use my voice with wisdom. I am using my voice in love. I am learning to understand how my words land on people`s hearts. I am a people builder. I want to help others get from pain to pleasure, by owning their voice and becoming the best version of themselves.

*In all thy ways acknowl-
edge him, and he shall
direct thy paths.*

Proverbs 3:6

[6] In all thy ways acknowledge him, and he shall direct thy paths.

CHAPTER 16

God Made a Way

*I*am sure now you have become intrigued, wondering who I am talking about. Well, it`s my brother Tony, Tony returned to the UK and lived in Birmingham for many years, but nobody knew his whereabouts. To be honest I couldn`t find him.

When I became a Christian I took a photo to Bishop Malcolm, for him to pray over the photo. Bishop told me to go and pray. My daughter was with me at the appointment. We were so disappointed, I thought, "Is he serious? Did he really tell me to go and pray? Isn`t that his job?" I became angry; "vex" as Jamaicans would say.

I complained to God, "How dear he tell me to go and pray? What do I know about praying; that`s why I went to him? I was so angry whenever I saw Bishop Malcolm coming my way, I would walk through the nearest door or turn back.

Little did I know that it was a setup from God. Yes, a set-up. That was God's way of getting me to pray. I eventually found Tony. After 10 years, he came to live with my son, daughter and me in London.

Tony passed away in 2002 in his sleep. I then became very angry with my parents, who both resided in Jamaica. It felt like I was left to pick up the pieces as if tony was my son. I thank God for my daughter Tasha and son Selvin who tolerated my mood. I thank God for Donna Parks, Theresa Beckles, Mary Abrahams and Valarie Morris. You all put up with my stubbornness and bad mood. It was as if I had died when Tony died.

I am choosing to use this chapter to show how I was able to prove God. Have you ever proved God? I was working part-time, and studying full time. There was no money to bury Tony. I could go to church, but I couldn't go to work. I stayed home praying singing and dancing unto the Lord.

One day after praying with my daughter because we could see that things didn't look good. The question was, "How am I going to bury Tony?"

I said to God. I don't care how you do it or who you use".

It was less than ten minutes that Bishop Malcolm telephoned and asked "How things were coming along". I said, "Not good, sir."

He told me to give him the number for the funeral parlour. He called and agreed to pay half the expenses. Pastor David Springer who conducted the funeral Service handed the money on the day of the funeral to the funeral director.

The funeral directors had so much compassion. For funerals, you are expected to pay all the costs before the day of the funeral. Well, I only paid half, Thanks to Bishop Malcolm.

I remember as if it was yesterday when Bishop Malcolm had finished talking to me, it felt like heaven had opened up to me. Money started flowing my way. I can honestly say that God didn't allow me to spend a penny towards Tony's funeral. To date, I am in awe. On the day of the funeral, the money I received as love seeds was more than what Bishop gave to me. I was able to give Bishop back his money. He did not want to take it. I explained to him, that before his telephone call to me my spirit was low, and I was in despair. Financially things were not looking hopeful for me to bury Tony. Bishop Malcolm's call to the funeral director enabled me to regain my confidence and sense of dignity. I regained physical strength and was able to see clearly again. I could focus on what needed to be done. I could give my brother the burial that he deserved.

Thank you, Theresa Beckles you guided me to contact The Department of Work and Pensions who then gave me enough money to pay the outstanding funeral cost. I just want to tell you that God is a provider, he has and will always be my Jehovah-Jireh (my provider). Genesis 22:14

Let your eyes look
straight ahead,
And your eyelids look
right before you.

Proverbs 4:25

CHAPTER 17

Reflections

$\mathcal{M}$y childhood reflection conversation with my mum on Thursday 29th April, 11.00 am UK time 5.00 am Jamaica time

I wanted to know what was I like as a child because I had vivid memories of what I was like below age 12 which is when I became interested in boys.

Mummy said that I was loved telling stories as a little girl, especially when she had come home from night work, and she was very tired. Mummy said I would always tell "never-ending stories"

Mummy said if she kept quiet! I would say "Mum are you listening?" she said I was around 4 years old. Mummy said my dad didn`t have the time to listen to me because I only told one story "over and over like a machine" she said my story about little children. Mummy said I always wanted her to have more children so I would have my own playgroup.

I don`t like working alone, I like teamwork even though I can work alone. At times I need quietness to think, read and write.

Hearing mummy talk was helping me because I have always liked writing. Writing and reading at primary school was what I liked best. I was scared of maths, but no one knew. I was scared. As an adult, I am grateful for technology.

Mummy said I was always singing and skipping, instead of just walking. My favourite nursery rhyme was "Here we go Looby loo" Nursery Rhyme By Sper Simple songs. I thought my mum had made this up.

I now realise I was a little conversationalist and this manifested in my adult life. While on the phone talking with a male friend for a while, he eventually said, "Who phoned who?" I had taken over the conversation and was doing all the talking. It was a nice feeling because I had learnt something new about myself, I liked to talk and to encourage people.

Mummy said there was a stage in my adult life when I wouldn`t talk to her, she said it was as if I didn`t have any time for her. Mummy went on to say I was going through my angry season. There was a season when I didn`t want to hear my voice because it felt like I was talking in vain, it was so painful.

I recall asking my mum in 2019 while on holiday in Jamaica what I was like as a little girl, she did say that I liked telling stories. I didn`t make a connection with the age or the fact that I liked writing and reading.

On 22nd April 2021, while doing prayer silence with Emelia my prayer partner (my Spiritual Daughter), I sensed the Lord saying, "You are a Narrator". I thought WOW!

I was becoming aware that I liked reading aloud. I noticed that I liked emphasizing my words when reading. I am a storyteller.

I shared with my mum that parents and grandparents need to notice the gifts and skills in their children. I was destined to be a public speaker and author.

Mummy and I spoke about me speaking through my bright colours, and she reminded me of a pair of blue shoes she bought for my cousin Audrey and me. My cousin Audrey always talked about the blue shoes.

As we reflected on my childhood, on her saying. "Children should be seen and not heard", I wondered if it was because I spoke too much as a child. I now know that adults in the 1950s said "Children should be seen and not heard", so that children would know their place, and not speak out of turn. On 19th July 2021, my mum confirmed that her grandmother had said it to her. Parents and grandparents let us be mindful of what we pass onto the next generation, our assignment is to empower them to become the best version of themselves.

Mummy said red and white were colours I wore as a little girl to a wedding as a flower girl, aged 6. White dress with red trimmings, red and white hat, red shoes and red handbag. This is no different from how I dress now, as red and white are the colours I wear for the events that I host.

Mummy and I spoke about the stripped jumper I wore to school instead of my white school blouse, blue cardigan and red tie when I wanted her attention. It was red, yellow, green, black, blue. I was being "very loud" in my colours but nobody heard me. So, it was "very silent". My teacher at secondary was supposed to pull me up, for not wearing my school uniform. Well that's what I expected, isn't that what you would expect a teacher to do. I expected her to call you mummy.

I told mummy that as a young woman I wore red because I was saying "keep off" to people. I was sending a clear message. After talking to my Pastor Yvonne Brookes she helped me to understand I was saying "keep off" to people, I thought it was a way to protect myself because I only wanted my mum's attention. She explained that as an adult I knew how to give but not receive.

I could see mummy enjoyed talking about my childhood. We had a bond when I was a little girl, I got her attention. She said she couldn't say shut up to me, but in her mind, she wanted to. Mummy said she wanted to tell me to shut up because I was telling the same story.

Mummy said I would always sit on her bed while she was laying down, in her mind she was saying "Not again! Oh my god." She couldn't express how painful it was then, but now she can. She said I would always say "Mummy can I tell you a story?"

On reflection, if she had told me to shut up, it would have hurt my feelings. Without her realising she did get me to shut, due to her busy lifestyle it didn't allow her to recognise, that as a little girl I wasn't getting the full attention from her.

I don't know if you remember the special moment's with your mum, sharing a box of chicken dinner with my mum while I sat under the counter of her shop in Jamaica was a special time for me, that dinner was just for us. I felt so special.

Arise, shine; For your light has come!

Isaiah 60:1 (NKJV)

Epilogue

*W*OW! WOW! WOW! the key to happiness lies within you. Satisfaction, personal success and the wonderful feeling of power and effectiveness are what I extend to you, my dear reader. Choosing to develop new habits can release you to take off the mask and face yourself. Help you to be honest with yourself while you learn to be your own liberator. We have to be honest that we are often the one that has limited ourselves by the narrative we embraced as a result of negative self-chatter and disbelief in ourselves.

Owning your voice; standing in your truth and becoming the best version of yourself, is a gift you owe yourself. Take some time to be kind to yourself. Embrace your uniqueness, no more excuses. Look in the mirror, have a good talk with yourself. Forgive yourself for your past mistakes make some new commitments to yourself for tomorrow. I know one day you will be thankful for the new self-love experience and transformation that it brings.

Don`t ask for permission to be you, because you already are you. Learn to celebrate yourself. You are unique there will never be another you. Learn to talk to yourself. No, it`s not a sign of madness, it`s a way to liberate yourself. As you hear yourself you learn to love and appreciate yourself, that`s what happened to me.

My reader, I encourage you to take that step, read yourself as you listen to yourself, and know the world is waiting to hear you.

Testimonials

Tasha Peeters

To my darling mother, I am so proud of your growth and personal achievement. You amaze me with your strength and tenacity. Keep reaching for your goals. The sky is the limit.

Tasha Peeters, Daughter.
Family Law Coach TP, LLB(Hons) Law
GCilex

Emelia Aimey, Teacher

When you meet a person, who talks with the same fervency as they walk, who has a determination to keep learning and then share the learning with others, you need to pay attention to that person and glean what you can – quickly, as there is no need to reinvent any wheel!!!

Pauline-Elizabeth (I know her as Mum P) is a woman who has chosen to speak her truth. The truth of realising that your past has helped to shape your present, and lessons learned from this journey can propagate you to walking in your God-given destiny. However, not learning, will leave you unfulfilled, frustrated and broken. Read the book, learn some truths and share what you discover. I know this is what Mum P understands can help you set yourself free by God's grace.

Emelia Aimey – Daughter by Design.

Beatrice Whyte

I have known Sis P for many years, I have had the privilege of attending most of her forums/prayer events.

Her events/book has enlightened and enriched me as a person to handle situations with dignity and respect. She tells her story so open and transparent but with that special love. Her story is one that allows me to know and understand that restoration can and does take place. Her events/book has given me that special tool that I can reflect on.

Thank you for being the transparent person you are. Parents like myself will have the tools to be able to nourish their children to the best of their ability and so much more because of it.

Wife, Mother to 4, Registered nurse.

Thank you, Sister P.

Shaneeka Williams

Pauline-Elizabeth, who I know as aunty, has written this book to also help young people Own their Voice. Aunty is able to put her heart on paper. She has also made it possible for me an 11-year-old girl to join the book club and start writing my book. I am grateful because I don`t have to hide my pain like aunty did at the age of 11. Thank you, aunty. This book is a must-read that can help you to know that you can tell your story. I am an 11-year-old girl.

Theresa Beckles

Pauline-Elizabeth, as much as she may believe that she has been hiding in the background, in my mind that has been far from the truth. She has always been faithful in her devotional and prayer life; consistent and focused on what she believes in.

Even when she was overlooked, she continued steadfastly in prayer and pressing forwards to become that voice crying in the wilderness making way for others.

May God continue to truly bless and anoint her on her journey as she unlocks the doors for many others owning their voices.

A voice crying in the wilderness will unlock many doors for many who have believed a lie that they 'are not worthy', 'not enough', and 'not loved', learn to love themselves and see the true beauty that God has created in them.

Theresa Beckles,
Counsellor/Mentor Founder of Exclusively You events.

Bishop Vivienne Downes

I am humbled to be asked by my spiritual daughter Pauline-Elizabeth to write this testimonial.

I met Pauline-Elizabeth at church and from the moment we met I was drawn to her. We engaged in a conversation about the way she worshipped which I thought was awesome. I am not sure how she became a part of my life and I became one of her Spiritual Mothers

When I met Pauline-Elizabeth, on the outside she looked very brave and confident I thought. She headed a Prayer Ministry and as time went by the Lord instructed Pauline-Elizabeth to do a Prayer Conference.

We discussed what needed to be done, however, she was not feeling confident to be one of the speakers. I encouraged her to trust God, go ahead and do 'Thus saith the Lord'. Pauline-Elizabeth spoke at the conference and there she found her voice. Each time there was an event I would give her feedback and on what she needed to work on. I truly love working with Pauline-Elizabeth because she`s very obedient and always listens to hear instructions from God about what she needs to do especially in her spiritual life.

I know God has blessed Pauline-Elizabeth with Grace and Favour. I am really proud of her and how she`s improved in her confidence and is now Owning her Voice and Speaking her Truth. I believe without a shadow of a doubt that this book will empower and encourage anyone who reads it to Own their Voice and Speak their Truth.

God bless you my Spiritual Daughter Pauline-Elizabeth.

Peter Nembhard, Senior pastor of Arc Church

In this book, Pauline-Elizabeth gives us exposure to the dark nights of her soul. She reaches back and shows us God`s redemption of her brokenness and how he can take broken people and use them for his glory.

This is a must-read for anyone who thinks that they are beyond the reach and love of God and that God cannot use them. Well done, Pauline-Elizabeth!

Theslyn Whyte, Nurse

I have known Pauline-Elizabeth for more than 5 years. She loves to encourage us to find our voice and get to know ourselves. She shares her life story freely so we can learn and lead fulfilling lives. She does not have a loud voice or tone, however, when she speaks, we listen.

Some years ago, as part of a course, she was pursuing, she asked whether she could mentor my teenage son. I agreed to this, however was hesitant as I thought – what could a 40+-year-old female teach my child. Later I was reminded that she is the mother of a now-adult male. Knowing this and the way in which Pauline-Elizabeth interacts increased my confidence and relieved my worry regarding her mentoring my son. My son has since completed an Apprenticeship and is employed.

Thank you, Pauline-Elizabeth.

Inez Anderson, Support Worker

This book is in reference to Pauline-Elizabeth. She is a member of the Arc Church Cedars Senior Group. Her book is about her life journey and the struggles she went through while growing up. She was born in the UK, her mother originated from Jamaica. They did not have a good mother and daughter relationship but God is so good, they both now enjoy one.

This book is a true testimony of her struggle and her strong faith in God. Well, Pauline-Elizabeth, all the best in the launching of your book *A Voice Crying in the Wilderness.*

Ena Hyatt

Formally a Primary school Teacher, presently Elder, Justice of the Peace

Redeem how I love to proclaim it,
Redeem by the blood of the Lamb,
Redeem through His infinite mercy
His child and forever I am,

Redeem I am so happy in Jesus

no language my rapture can tell

I know that the light of his presence

with me doth continually dwell

Fanny Jane Crosby (1820-1915)

I am sure these are some words my niece can borrow from the song by Fanny Crosby, as she makes her journey through her book.

In the past without God, we lived far from God and were children of anger hopeless and aimless in life. God has found us and has given us life in Christ. He forgave us our sins because of His love and not of our merits, because we are saved, we must do the deeds God wants us to practice. Prayer is powerful, in the conflict against the enemy. Prayer allows us to know God`s will.

Many years ago, my niece would find it difficult to reach out to her mother. There was no mother and daughter relationship. Being in the middle person of Aunt and sister made me very uncomfortable. Whenever my sister reached out to me I always consoled her and encouraged her not to have any bitterness in her heart for her daughter, but she should pray and ask God to turn her around. I always prayed for God to intervene before her mother die, and I was confident that he would.

I always encouraged my niece to ask God to give her a forgiving spirit. Whenever my niece came to Jamaica on holiday, she never had the courage to stay at her mother's home. This also made me feel very uncomfortable. I believe in prayer and I never stopped praying for my sister and niece relationship to be restored.

I can remember the time when my niece told me she would be coming to Jamaica and staying with her mother. I felt so happy and thanked God for answered prayers. That holiday was a turning point in their lives. The relationship has blossomed into a great friendship. Thank God for giving men technology. Every day they are both on the phone for hours speaking to each other and always looking into each other's eyes.

My sister is now a happier person and even looks twenty years younger. My niece Pauline Elizabeth Grant is now blooming in the Lord and has become a lighter person. That heavy burden she was carrying for her mother is now at the foot of the cross and she is happy in the Lord.

She is now able to encourage others to take their burdens to the Lord in prayer. I would like to encourage everyone who reads her book to allow the Holy Spirit to lead us to do the work God wants us to do. According to Jeremiah the question "Is there anything too hard for the Lord". (Jeremiah 32:27(NIV) The answer is "No" Nothing is too hard for the Lord to do. May the spirit of God continue with all of us.

About the Author

*P*auline-Elizabeth wrote this book to inspire you to own your voice and break Generational silence. As an author who has fallen in love with her passion to speak her truth, she believes you also have a book in you.

Breaking the silence can start with you owning your voice. Pauline-Elizabeth said it is time to take off the mask, as for years she was scared to let people know that there are gaps in her knowledge.

Pauline-Elizabeth said being vulnerable is a risk, a risk which she feels is necessary to take. She said it will take one person to speak their truth to enable personal breakthroughs, to bring healing and also clarity to misunderstanding in broken families. She is the product of a broken family.

Pauline-Elizabeth is holding her hand up by acknowledging that no one held her back in life. It was her own negative chatter that she believed about herself. She said we must strive to be the best version of ourselves.

On the 3rd Sunday of each month, Pauline-Elizabeth hosts a Women's Empowerment Forum called "A Voice Crying in the Wilderness". It`s a safe environment via zoom where women share and hear stories. Women can grow from pain to pleasure, while they speak their truth.

Pauline-Elizabeth is a Transformational Coach. Her coaching business is called "Family Restorative Clinic". She also runs a group workshop on Zoom called "Own Your Voice". Her mantra is "Own Your Voice, Stand in Your Truth, and be the best version of yourself".

Services

*P*auline-Elizabeth is a Transformational Coach, founder of 'Family Restorative Clinic' (FRC) Coaching Business, Coordinator of R.O.O.T.S Prayer Ministry. Pauline-Elizabeth is passionate about seeing people experience their own AH-HA moment for personal development and transformation from the inside to the outside reflecting their confidence.

Email: paulinegrant858@gmail.com, or coachpaulineelizabeth@gmail.com,

Facebook: Pauline Elizabeth

Instagram: @coachpaulineelizabeth

Tashie's Place

*M*y future project is: Tashie's Place represents a house in Jamaica, a safe home that can accommodate four teenage girls supporting them to access education without turning to prostitution for financial gain. It is in memory of my spiritual daughter Tashie she came into my life at age 13, she died after contracting aids at the age of 23 in 1999 I will be looking for sponsors to help bring support to the girls. I am grateful to Malachi Talabi, Nana Jones, Rose Steel and Opal, for believing in me and sowing a seed of faith into my project. I believe God is showing me when he gives the vision, he will make the provision.

My present legacy is 'R.O.O.T.S Prayer Ministry' which is the umbrella for my spiritual life, which started in 2001 with a Prayer Breakfast. With my team, we have engaged in PUSH Night Vigils, several prayer conferences, a Prayer summit, a Prayer retreat.

'Let Go And Let God' Sunday evening meetings, giving women and men the opportunity to show off their God-given talents.

'Soldiers for Christ' (SFC) Wednesday lunchtime prayer meeting.

'A Voice Crying in the Wilderness' Zoom forum gives women a plat-form to tell and hear stories, women can take off the mask in a safe space

'Family Restorative Clinic'(FRC) is the umbrella for my coaching busi-ness, which started with the "Own Your Voice" Women`s empower-ment workshop in 2021. The focus of FRC is working with 1 to many people in a venue, group sessions or online packages, because we are now in digital time, which enables me to serve people near or far

References

Super Simple Songs, *Childhood Nursery Rhyme* "Here we go Looby Loo". Internet cited on 04.08.2021 at: https://www.youtube.com/watch?v=EHaoEKcuX0g

Angelou, Maya (1986) "I rise", Random House, USA.

Printed in Great Britain
by Amazon

77791340R00068